AF226144

FOOD SCIENCE

BY CHRISTA HOGAN

Essential Library
An Imprint of Abdo Publishing
abdobooks.com

ABDOBOOKS.COM

Published by Abdo Publishing, a division of ABDO, PO Box 398166, Minneapolis, Minnesota 55439. Copyright © 2025 by Abdo Consulting Group, Inc. International copyrights reserved in all countries. No part of this book may be reproduced in any form without written permission from the publisher. Essential Library™ is a trademark and logo of Abdo Publishing.

Printed in China.
102024
012025

Cover Photos: Costfoto/Future Publishing/Getty Images (front); Shutterstock Images (back)
Interior Photos: Costfoto/Future Publishing/Getty Images, 1; Heidi Besen/Shutterstock Images, 5; Shutterstock Images, 6, 16, 20, 29, 35, 58, 65; Gado/Archive Photos/Getty Images, 9; Jeff Greenberg/Universal Images Group/Getty Images, 11; Inside Creative House/Shutterstock Images, 19; John Carl D'Annibale/Albany Times Union/Hearst Newspapers/Getty Images, 23; Dragon Images/Shutterstock Images, 26; Liz Hafalia/San Francisco Chronicle/Hearst Newspapers/Getty Images, 32; Sazhnieva Oksana/Shutterstock Images, 38 (fat); Skyline Graphics/Shutterstock Images, 38 (sugar, salt); Marc Elias/Shutterstock Images, 41; Tada Images/Shutterstock Images, 44; Peggy Greb/USDA/Science Source, 47; Edwin Remsberg/Alamy, 50–51; Christopher Dilts/Bloomberg/Getty Images, 55; Philipp Schulze/dpa/picture alliance/Getty Images, 61; Justin Sullivan/Getty Images News/Getty Images, 68; Joe Raedle/Getty Images News/Getty Images, 71; Juan Mabromata/AFP/Getty Images, 74; Christophe Archambault/AFP/Getty Images, 79; Kevork Djansezian/AP Images, 81; Fabrice Coffrini/AFP/Getty Images, 84; Romeo Gacad/AFP/Getty Images, 89; Arife Karakum/Anadolu/Getty Images, 92; Oliver Morin/AFP/Getty Images, 95; Ma Xiuxiu/VCG/China News Service/Getty Images, 96; Kyodo News Stills/Getty Images, 99

Editor: Kari Cornell
Series Designer: Maggie Villaume

Library of Congress Control Number: 2024938297

PUBLISHER'S CATALOGING-IN-PUBLICATION DATA
Names: Hogan, Christa, author.
Title: Food science / by Christa Hogan
Description: Minneapolis, Minnesota: ABDO Publishing, 2025 | Series: Fascinating food | Includes online resources and index.
Identifiers: ISBN 9781098295295 (lib. bdg.) | ISBN 9798384916291 (ebook)
Subjects: LCSH: Nutrition--Health aspects--Juvenile literature. | Clinical nutrition--Juvenile literature. | Food science--Juvenile literature. | Food technology--Juvenile literature. | Food--Microbiology--Juvenile literature. | Genetically modified foods--Juvenile literature. | Food chemistry--Juvenile literature.
Classification: DDC 664--dc23

CONTENTS

THE WORLD OF FOOD SCIENCE

The supermarket hums with shoppers pushing carts full of their favorite foods. These foods might include ripe tomatoes, breakfast cereals, and cans of peaches, beans, and soup. Shoppers may think about how long these foods will take to prepare, how they will taste, and how much they will cost. It is unlikely, though, that the shoppers are considering the hours of research and experimentation that went into the items in their carts.

Long before groceries hit supermarket shelves, food scientists spend many hours asking the same questions as shoppers. How will the food taste? How fast can consumers prepare it? How much will the product cost? The answers they discover through research and experimentation help determine which products shoppers find on store shelves.

According to surveys, the average US adult visits the grocery store six times each month.

People can pickle many kinds of foods by soaking them in vinegar and salt inside a sealed jar. The vinegar's high acidity prevents pickled food from going bad.

WHAT IS FOOD SCIENCE?

In 2022, the average supermarket carried 31,530 items, many of which were developed by food scientists.[1] Food science is the study of food using chemistry, biochemistry, physics, microbiology, nutrition, agriculture, engineering, and other disciplines. Every day, food scientists work to make food safe, nutritious, appealing, and convenient for consumers. They consider the best ways to produce, process, and preserve food.

Different types of food scientists play their own roles in the process of bringing nutritious food to market safely. Food engineers help the food industry find new ways to process and store products. Food microbiologists study how to preserve the food safely. Food chemists produce new tastes, textures, and appearances that make products more appealing to consumers. Food scientists are also instrumental in meeting the world's growing demand for food.

By 2050, the world's population will increase to an estimated nine billion people.[2] This will put an additional strain on already challenged environments and food systems. With this in mind, food scientists are searching for more sustainable and ethical food sources.

FOOD SCIENCE BEGINNINGS

During the French Revolutionary wars (1792–1799), the government offered 12,000 francs to anyone who could devise a way to preserve food for the French army as it traveled throughout Europe to invade other countries.[3] Popular methods of preserving at the time included drying, smoking, fermenting, and pickling, but no method worked well all the time. Foods could still become

MUMMIFIED MEAT

In ancient Egypt, birds and fish were readily available across all levels of society. However, meat from mammals was enjoyed mostly by the wealthy elite or during special occasions. This was because of the cost of raising and slaughtering livestock and the difficulty of hunting wild game.

Egyptians preserved meat through drying, salting, and smoking. Food was also mummified for use in funeral rituals and burials for the elite. Archaeologists found 48 wooden cases of butchered beef and poultry buried with King Tutankhamun.[4] Mummified meat was wrapped in bandages and sealed in a layer of animal fat or coated in plant resin.

contaminated, and spoilage was a big economic expense. Foodborne illnesses were a major cause of preventable deaths during this time. This was especially a problem with contaminated milk, which was responsible for spreading diseases such as tuberculosis, diphtheria, and typhoid fever.

Nicolas Appert won the prize with his development of the canning process. Though Appert was a candymaker, he turned to wine-making methods for inspiration. Appert placed food in jars and heated them in boiling water to kill the bacteria and microorganisms, then vacuum sealed the jars as they cooled to prevent them from being contaminated by other bacteria. In 1810, after Appert's discovery, British inventor Peter Durand began preserving food in containers made of tin and other metals.

Louis Pasteur

French chemist Louis Pasteur was born in Dole, France, on December 27, 1822. He had an interest in chemistry and earned his doctorate at the École Normale Supérieure in Paris in 1847. While conducting research at the University of Lille, he made a discovery that would later revolutionize food preparation and preservation and pave the way for a safer food supply. Pasteur developed pasteurization, a process that uses heat to kill harmful bacteria. He did it mainly to prevent the spoiling and waste of French wines and beers, an economic source of national pride.

Before Pasteur's work, scientists were unfamiliar with the role that microbes played in the fermentation and spoiling of food. Pasteur understood that bacteria made their homes in foods, especially in liquids. He knew that these bacteria contributed to foods' decomposition.

On April 20, 1862, Pasteur conducted his first test, using a method of heating liquids to just below the boiling point and then cooling them. This would destroy harmful bacteria without affecting the taste or quality of the beverage. Pasteur's simple method greatly improved human health and food safety around the world. His original method was soon adapted and expanded to meet a variety of needs in the food industry.

EARLY FOOD SAFETY

Although canning methods advanced food preservation, food safety remained an issue. If high enough temperatures weren't used, the container seal was weak, or the tin cans weren't heated long enough, the food inside would still spoil. Sometimes the spoilage was obvious once the container was opened.

Other times, however, the cans held invisible killers, including the bacterium *C. botulinum*. In environments with little oxygen, *C. botulinum* produces a deadly toxin that can't be seen, smelled, or tasted. It attacks the nervous system. Consumers suffering from the resulting illness, called botulism, experience difficulty breathing, seeing, and swallowing. They also experience muscle weakness and vomiting. If not treated quickly, symptoms can lead to paralysis and death.

Food safety concerns such as this eventually led to the creation of the Food and Drug Administration (FDA). The US government created the FDA in 1906 with the Pure Food and Drug Act. This law aimed to protect consumers from foods

> The toxin that causes botulism is so poisonous that one-millionth of a gram could kill a human.[5]

Government agencies may regulate the types of cans used for food, the temperature to which canned products are heated, and how long canned goods are heated.

that were mislabeled or adulterated. Adulterated foods are foods that include additives, coloring, or other substances that undermine the quality of the product. This was a step in the right direction, but food-based illnesses and deaths continued to happen.

From 1919 to 1920, 18 consumers in the United States died from botulism after eating canned black olives from California.[6] Fearing a backlash from the public and loss of profits, the National Canners Association and the California Canners League joined forces to find a solution. They created

COLD STORAGE

Prior to World War I (1914–1918), salads with fresh lettuce were enjoyed seasonally, usually with a variety known as butter lettuce. But with advancements in refrigerated shipping in the late 1910s and early 1920s, produce growers in sunny California could ship foods to consumers across the country in cities such as New York City and Chicago, Illinois. Iceberg lettuce fared best on the long, frigid journey. The robust, tightly bunched leaves meant it could be packed in ice and arrive at its destination still crisp and cool. An iceberg lettuce craze swept the nation. By 1925, consumers enjoyed iceberg lettuce salads year-round.

the Botulism Commission, a group of scientists dedicated to solving the food safety crisis. The commission created a rigorous set of practices for safe food preservation.

The canning industry embraced the new standards, and California state government agencies made sure food processing companies followed the rules. The standards helped keep consumers safe. Perhaps just as important, developing these standards forged relationships between the food industry, government agencies, and scientists that would set the foundation for the national regulation of food safety.

FOOD SCIENCE AND PUBLIC SAFETY

During the 1900s, technological advances, cultural changes, and shifting consumer demands gave rise to the food industry and the field of food science as it exists today. Soldiers fighting in World War I (1914–1918) and World War II (1939–1945), who had grown accustomed to eating foods preserved in tin cans, popularized their use for family meals once they returned home. Frozen dinners and packets of condiments were also developed for military use. Once the wars ended, factories that had once mass-produced these supplies for soldiers switched their focus to providing instant soups, cake mixes, and potato chips for consumers.

During the 1950s, the working middle class was growing rapidly around the world and moving in to more urban areas. Women entered the workforce, and working families wanted cheaper, packaged convenience foods they could prepare at home. New technologies made it possible for the food industry to meet consumers' shifting expectations.

Manufacturers of magnetron tubes, which had been used by the military for short-range radar technology, found ways to heat food with radio waves. In 1946, the first microwave ovens hit the market. Because of the massive size and expense of these early microwaves, restaurants were the primary customers.

By the 1960s, however, consumers were using smaller and more affordable models of microwaves in their home kitchens to heat ready-to-eat dinners. Refrigerators were also widely available by then, as well as large freezers that families could use to preserve frozen dinners. The development of plastic wrap and resealable plastic containers also helped consumers store meals and leftovers for longer periods.

Each of these advances required the work of highly trained scientists who helped companies create affordable, convenient, and safe products. Universities around the world responded by developing new academic programs that would train the experts the food industry needed. These early programs linked home economics, agriculture, and nutrition and would later become the field of food science.

FOOD SAFETY REGULATION

In the 1990s and early 2000s, consumers began to recognize the downsides of packaged and processed convenience foods. Processing was a good way to preserve foods, but it sometimes compromised their nutritional value by reducing fiber, vitamins, and minerals. Ingredients with lower nutrition quality were used to reduce cost. Salt, fat, and sugar were added to make products last longer, taste better, and look more appealing to consumers.

These ingredients also increased the calories and sodium in the products. Rates of diet-related diseases, such as type 2 diabetes, increased. Christopher Gardner studies the connection between diet and disease at Stanford University. He says, "Four of the top six killers are related to an inadequate diet, which in the US is probably largely due to convenient, safe, inexpensive food that we eat too much of."[7] Consumers, health officials, and government agencies questioned if the food industry cared more about profits than public health.

Today, many government agencies regulate food production, processing, and packaging. In addition to the FDA, which ensures the proper labeling of drugs and food products, the US Department of Agriculture (USDA) oversees the safety of meat, poultry,

SPACE FOOD

During the 1960s, the United States and the Soviet Union competed to achieve important firsts in human space exploration. This competition, which came to be called the Space Race, involved not only rockets and spacecraft but also the science of food preservation. To feed astronauts in space, food scientists developed new methods of preserving foods, including freeze-drying and thermostabilization. Freeze-drying is removing the water from the food before sealing it. Thermostabilization is similar to canning foods using heat in boiling water. The food is heated to kill bacteria, then stored in sealed pouches, cans, or cups called wet packs.

and egg products. The Centers for Disease Control and Prevention (CDC) tracks and investigates cases of foodborne illness. And the National Oceanic and Atmospheric Administration (NOAA) enforces standards for seafood. These agencies and others work with the food industry and health experts to continually improve the safety and quality of the nation's food supply.

Modern food scientists form the backbone of the food industry. Scientists trained in the fields of biology, nutrition, physics, chemistry, and agriculture help companies create new and exciting products that appeal to consumers' tastes and budgets—all while following health and safety guidelines. The balance between these demands creates a rewarding challenge for food scientists.

FOOD PROCESSING METHODS

Humans have always needed food to provide them with the energy to live. Because food begins to decay the moment it's harvested, humans have developed ways to process and preserve their food. As the planet's population continues to grow and the demand for convenience foods increases with it, scientists and manufacturers rely on more processing and preservation methods than ever before.

The phrase *food processing* refers to the methods and techniques used to turn ingredients such as meat, grains, and dairy into the food products sold in stores today. Processing methods range from familiar techniques used at home to more complex and industrialized approaches. When food is processed, it means that it has been cut, cleaned, chopped, ground, cooked, frozen, dried, mixed with

Chopping vegetables is one way that home cooks process
food to be eaten.

Canned vegetables have most of the same nutrients as fresh vegetables. These processed foods often have few added ingredients, although they may include additional salt or sugar.

other ingredients, or packaged. Humans have been milling, grinding, chopping, and washing food to prepare meals at home for thousands of years. These methods make foods safer and more appealing to eat. They minimally disrupt the nutritional content of the ingredients and do not require the use of industrial chemicals.

However, food that is mass-produced and shipped undergoes extensive processing and preservation to eliminate harmful bacteria and extend the product's shelf life. Processed food may have added flavors or preservatives that are approved for use in food. Often processed foods include added salt, fat, and sugar.

Not all foods are processed the same amount. A classification system called NOVA breaks foods into four groups. Unprocessed and minimally processed foods include those that are cut or served whole, such as avocados, carrots, or milk. Processed culinary ingredients are made from natural foods with minimal processing, such as olive oil or almond flour. Processed foods, such as canned tuna, are changed from their natural form, often by adding ingredients including oil, salt, or sugar. Ultra-processed foods (UPFs) contain many ingredients not found in nature, including artificial colors and flavors.

UPFs also include ingredients extracted from nature, such as hydrogenated fats and starches. Potato chips, packaged cookies, soft drinks, hot dogs, and deli meats are examples of UPFs. UPFs are produced using methods and machinery found only in factories.

WAYS TO PRESERVE FOODS

Many of the methods that food manufacturers use to preserve food are familiar to home cooks. Other methods

SUGAR, FAT, AND SALT

Scientists have studied the effects of sugar, fat, and salt on the brain. They found that fat and sugar in particular, both high in calories, produce strong reward signals in the brain. This means foods that contain fat and sugar make people feel good when they eat them. As a result, scientists began to study whether and how processed foods can become addictive to loyal consumers.

Meanwhile, consumers have become more proactive about their health. They are reading food labels before adding items to their carts. Consumers are also demanding healthier food choices with less added salt, sugar, and fat and fewer additives and chemicals.

are more complex and specific to the food industry. These methods include irradiation, pasteurization, pascalization, and encapsulation.

Irradiation involves treating food with radiation. It kills insects in imported tropical fruits, delays the ripening of bananas, prevents potatoes from sprouting eyes, and reduces harmful pathogens, including *Salmonella* and *Listeria*, in fresh fish. Irradiation doesn't use heat, so it preserves a food's nutritional properties.

During irradiation, food is placed on a conveyor belt that passes through a radiation chamber. In the chamber, beams containing low levels of ionizing radiation, including gamma rays, electron beams, and X-rays, are directed over the food. The radiation breaks the chemical bonds in mold and bacteria cells, killing the microorganisms.

Pasteurization kills many harmful microbes and stops enzymatic activity, which can change the texture and flavor of the product. This prolongs the product's shelf life by days or weeks. Pasteurization is used to preserve many foods, including milk, eggs, canned goods, and juices.

Milk may be pasteurized in large vats. In the most common method of pasteurization, milk is heated to 161 degrees Fahrenheit (72°C) for 15 seconds.

Pascalization, also called high-pressure processing, reduces microbial growth. The method is named after Blaise Pascal, a scientist who lived in the 1600s and studied how pressure affected fluids. During pascalization, food products are sealed inside a flexible container, such as a pouch or plastic bottle. The container is then loaded into a chamber that is filled with filtered water and placed under more than 87,000 pounds per square inch (600,000 kPa) of pressure.[1] The extreme pressure kills unwanted microorganisms, including mold and bacteria, in as little as 15 minutes, but not the spores that allow for the growth of new bacteria.

Pascalization is preferred for use in acidic foods and beverages, such as yogurts and orange juice, as spores cannot live in these foods due to the acidity. Pascalization retains a food's original taste and nutritional value. It also extends the shelf life of products by up to 30 days, reduces the need for preservatives or additives, and can be applied to food in its packaging, reducing the chance for cross contamination.[2]

Encapsulation uses a capsule to contain solids, liquids, or gases so they can be released later under certain conditions. These capsules are usually made of polysaccharides, proteins, or fats and are food grade. Most encapsulated foods are sprayed with these substances, which break down to release the ingredient at a certain temperature or in a specific environment.

Encapsulation is used to mask ingredients that might smell or taste unpleasant. It can also protect desirable aspects of a food, including vitamins or helpful bacteria, and prevent them from breaking down during processing. And encapsulation is used to contain flavoring agents, artificial sweeteners, coloring, preservatives, and leavening agents, such as yeast, baking soda, or baking powder. For example, manufacturers use encapsulation in cake mixes to contain baking powder and baking soda, which give cakes their light and fluffy texture. These ingredients are released when water is added to the cake mix.

MICROBIOLOGY OF FOOD PRESERVATION

Consumers often take for granted that the food they purchase in stores is safe. However, foodborne illness, also called food poisoning, is still a serious threat to human health. According to the magazine *Consumer Reports*, the top ten foods that are most likely to cause illness outbreaks are ground beef, turkey, chicken, deli meats and cheeses, onions, papayas, peaches, cantaloupes, flour, and leafy greens.

Food poisoning occurs when people eat or drink something contaminated by harmful bacteria or chemicals. Food and drinks can become contaminated at any point in the production process, including growth, shipping, processing, and preparation.

The CDC estimates that each year in the United States, 48 million people get food poisoning. Of that number, more than 128,000 are hospitalized and approximately 3,000 people die.[3]

Washing produce is one way to remove harmful germs that may cause foodborne illnesses.

The most common foodborne illnesses are caused by *Salmonella*, *E. coli*, and *Listeria*. These illnesses cause symptoms including stomach cramps, diarrhea, vomiting, and fever.

James Rogers is the director of food safety research and testing at *Consumer Reports*. He says, "Any consumer can become sick from contaminated food. However, the immunocompromised, the older consumer, younger children, and the unborn are all at higher risk for the after-effects of foodborne illnesses."[4] Food scientists play an important role in preventing foodborne illnesses and protecting the food supply.

Food microbiologists study microbes, including bacteria, yeast, molds, and viruses, that cause foodborne illnesses and food spoilage. Microbiologists manipulate the acidity, moisture, oxygen levels, or temperature of a food to prevent harmful microorganisms from growing. They may help develop guidelines for removing and minimizing contamination on equipment and workers, in safe storage, and in distribution.

Microbiologists also come up with ways to extend foods' shelf lives and keep food from spoiling by using nonhazardous microorganisms. For instance, they determine the ideal temperatures to prevent spoilage or contamination through cooking or refrigerating a food. They also work to reduce the amount of moisture in dried goods to prevent mold and yeast growth, and they use salt and acids, such as vinegar, for pickling and fermenting to eliminate bacteria.

WITCHY WHEAT

In 1691, girls in Salem, Massachusetts, experienced convulsions, slurred speech, hallucinations, and a strange rash, which some in the community called "the Devil's mark." Baffled area doctors blamed witchcraft. In the following eight months, dozens of villagers were tried for witchcraft, and more than 20 people and two dogs were executed.[5] Scientists and historians now speculate that the girls' symptoms were caused by eating rye bread contaminated by the toxic fungus ergot. Centuries later, ergot would be used to produce the hallucinogen LSD.

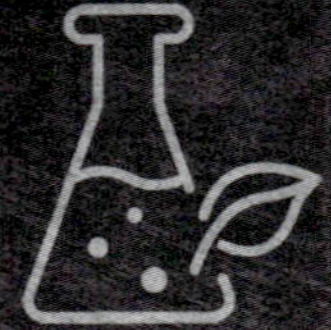

CHAPTER THREE

FOOD CHEMISTRY

People may not like to think about chemicals in their food. However, chemicals and chemical reactions are present in almost every aspect of how food reaches people's plates—from growing and preparing to cooking and preserving. In fact, chemistry plays a large role in how food tastes and what it looks like.

One major way that chemistry shows up in food science is through the use of food additives. Food additives aren't new to the human diet. For example, humans have been using salt to preserve food and limit bacterial growth for centuries. These days, food additives have become more complex, synthetic, and controversial. Food additives can be used in foods to stabilize, preserve, improve, or correct the final product. Additives often lower the cost of a product because the food does not need to be shipped as

Many candies are made with food dyes to achieve their brightly colored appearance. Although some dyes are natural, many are artificial.

quickly or stored under specific conditions, such as in a refrigerator, that may be expensive. Food manufacturers use additives in virtually every processed beverage and food product available today.

STABILIZERS

Stabilizers are added to foods to maintain or improve the texture as well as the physical and chemical characteristics. Emulsifiers and anticaking agents are two common kinds of stabilizing additives. Emulsifiers help two or more liquids mix that wouldn't normally join together. Lecithin is a common natural emulsifier found in egg yolks and soybean oil. It and other emulsifiers are added to foods such as mayonnaise, ice cream, and margarine to prevent separation of the oil and water. Emulsifier molecules have a polar head attracted to water and a nonpolar tail attracted to oil. In an oil-and-water solution, the polar end pairs with water molecules while the nonpolar end connects to oil molecules, binding the two substances together.

Anticaking agents prevent dry products from clumping or absorbing moisture. Food scientists use anticaking agents in dry baking mixes, hot cocoa packets, and dry soup mixes. Silica, also called silicon dioxide, is a commonly used anticaking agent. Silica occurs naturally in quartz, plants, and water. Silica attaches to food particles and prevents them from sticking together.

MODIFIERS

Modifiers are food additives that change the sensory experience of a product, including the way it looks, tastes, or smells. Common modifiers include coloring agents, sweeteners, and aromatic substances. Flavor chemists also add flavoring agents to many beverages and snacks. Sweeteners and other flavorings are often needed to balance sourness or other unpleasant tastes.

Flavoring agents are either created in a lab or extracted from natural sources. Natural flavors are created using infusions and essential oils made from natural elements, such as spices, fruits, vegetables, or meat. To make infusions, these items are soaked in oil or alcohol, which absorbs

XANTHAN GUM

Xanthan gum is a common food additive that thickens, adds texture, and keeps ingredients in place. It is considered nontoxic and biodegradable. Xanthan gum thickens once it reaches the digestive tract, which may slow digestion of foods. It also provides little to no nutritional value. The average person consumes less than a gram of xanthan gum a day, more than 20 times the amount that is proven to be safe.[1] The FDA places no limits on the amount of xanthan gum used in food products. It is commonly used in salad dressings, ice cream, gluten-free flours, juices, toothpaste, sauces, and syrups.

Food scientists may smell, taste, and mix chemicals to achieve a desired flavor.

the flavors. The vanilla extract used in many baked goods is created by soaking vanilla beans in alcohol.

Other flavors are artificial. To create artificial flavors, food scientists called flavorists taste the food they are trying to match and write down words that describe that flavor. They might describe a strawberry as sweet, jammy, and slightly citrusy. Flavorists and chemists study the chemical makeup of a natural strawberry and find the set of chemical compounds that matches the flavor, testing many combinations along the way.

Food companies turn to artificial additives, also known as nature-identical additives, instead of natural ones for several reasons. Artificial flavors may be more affordable for consumers and more profitable for the manufacturer. To make flavoring using real cherries, for example, would take a lot of cherries and a great deal of processing time.

The cost of the cherries and the expense to process the fruit would make the flavoring much more expensive than creating the artificial flavor in a lab.

Artificial flavors also tend to stay more stable during processes such as cooking and heating. This results in a better flavor in the end. Or the flavor agent may help replace a taste sensation lost by reducing salt, fat, or other elements in order to improve the nutrition of a product.

ARE FOOD ADDITIVES SAFE?

Natural and artificial food additives are regulated by government agencies. But consumers and health advocates are voicing concern. Elizabeth K. Dunford was a nutrition researcher at the University of North Carolina at Chapel Hill. She says, "Our research clearly shows that the proportion of ultra-processed foods

VANILLA: REAL OR ARTIFICIAL

Vanilla is made from an orchid that is notoriously difficult to grow. But artificial vanilla, called vanillin, can be made using compounds found in glucose, lignin from wood, or an enzymatic process, a chemical reaction in living organisms that can be done in a lab. While vanillin may not have as complex a flavor as real vanilla, home cooks often prefer it in their finished products. This is because the flavor in real vanilla doesn't stand up to high-temperature baking, leaving cookies and cakes tasting bland. Vanillin is also less expensive and easier to produce.

with additives in Americans' shopping carts increased significantly between 2001 and 2019. . . . These findings give us reason for concern, given the growing evidence linking high consumption of processed foods with adverse health outcomes."[2]

In the United States, the FDA regulates common ingredients and additives in food products. Any ingredient used in foods that are sold in the United States must be classified by the FDA as generally recognized as safe (GRAS). GRAS ingredients are those that have been previously used in food and shown through studies available to the public to be safe for human consumption.

Examples of GRAS ingredients include everything from the basic makings of a salad dressing, such as canola oil and vinegar, to the nitrates added to deli meats as a preservative. A nonprofit organization called the Environmental Working Group advocates for a healthy environment. It has published a list of additives called the Dirty Dozen Guide to Food Chemicals. These are chemicals added to food that it says consumers should avoid. Some of these include potassium bromate, which is added to baked goods; BHA, a chemical used to preserve cured meats; and TBHQ, a preservative used in Pop-Tarts and other foods. Potassium bromate

BHT is a chemical commonly found in cereals including Cap'n Crunch. Some studies have linked BHT to negative health effects.

and BHA may cause cancer, while TBHQ may interfere with the effectiveness of vaccines. Food manufacturers can use only additives approved by the FDA for use in food manufacturing.

GETTING FDA APPROVAL

When food manufacturers want to use a new food additive, they must petition the FDA for approval. The food company must show scientific evidence of the proposed additive's acceptable daily intake, or the amount that's safe for a person to eat each day over a lifetime. The FDA also considers the outcomes of a person eating far more than average amounts. The FDA reviews the petition, and if meat or poultry are involved, it consults with the USDA. If an additive is approved, the FDA specifies how the additive can be used and how it should be identified on food labels. It also sets a limit on the amount of additive that can be used in a product.

But critics point out flaws in this system. The scientific data provided to the FDA for review is sometimes written by the employees of food manufacturers and paid analysts, who may be biased sources. Food manufacturers argue that additives are extensively studied. They also say additives are necessary to make the modern food supply safer, more sustainable, and more equitable. In the years since the GRAS law was passed in 1958, however, the FDA has been overwhelmed by the number of ingredients to be reviewed and has lacked the resources to confirm that the data presented by food companies is accurate.

The American Academy of Pediatrics (AAP) made an urgent statement calling for the FDA to reform its approval process in 2018. The AAP cited growing research that consuming food additives puts children, and especially lower income consumers who rely on less expensive and less nutritional foods, at higher risk for endocrine disruption.

This is a shift in normal hormone levels within the body. It can reduce the response of the immune system after a vaccination and cause other health issues. Children are more at risk because their developing bodies are unable to process chemicals as efficiently as those of adults. The AAP's recommendations to the FDA included reviewing food packaging ingredients, revising the approval of GRAS to include toxicity testing, and retesting the more than 10,000 chemicals allowed in foods today.[3]

UPFs AND ADDITIVES

UPFs include few natural ingredients, are highly processed, and tend to contain high levels of food additives. UPFs make up 60 percent of Americans' food intake.[4] Many of these items are foods children may consume on a regular basis. They include candies, sodas, sweet or salty snacks, frozen pizzas, hot dogs, chicken or fish nuggets, and many gluten-free snacks, vegan meat alternatives, and food products designed for babies.

Other Names for Fat, Sugar, and Salt

FAT

Butter, margarine, animal fat, vegetable oil/fat, shortening, dripping, ghee, lard, palm oil, tallow, suet, copha, coconut, coconut oil, coconut cream, butterfat, milk solids, chocolate, monoglycerides, diglycerides, triglycerides

SUGAR

Sucrose, fructose, maltose, glucose, dextrose, lactose, honey, golden syrup, treacle, corn syrup, fruit juice concentrate, malt, malt extract, molasses, palm sugar

SALT

Baking soda, baking powder, sodium, sodium bicarbonate, monosodium glutamate, rock salt, vegetable salt, soy sauce

Consumers looking for added fat, sugar, and salt won't always find them under these common names. For example, sugar comes in many forms. Manufacturers may include sugar in the form of sucrose, glucose, or corn syrup. This chart includes many of the terms used for fat, sugar, and salt, along with ingredients that contain a lot of those nutrients. Not all of these ingredients are unhealthy or unnatural.

The debate over whether food additives are needed to create delicious and safe food continues. Health experts, the food industry, and government agencies will continue to debate policy for a safe, sustainable, and nutritious food supply. Meanwhile, consumers can avoid UPFs by looking at food labels for high amounts of saturated and trans fats, sodium, sugar, and additives and low levels of nutrients such as fiber, protein, vitamins, and minerals. Trans fats are plant oils that have been chemically processed to be solid at room temperature. These fats raise harmful LDL cholesterol in the body, which can contribute to heart disease.

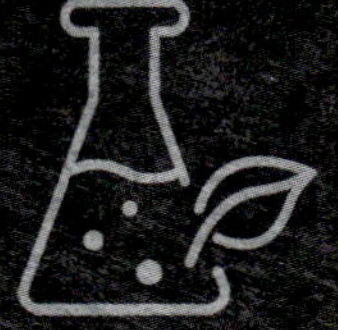

CHAPTER FOUR

THE INDUSTRIALIZED FOOD SYSTEM

Over the past 200 years, the way in which food is produced in the United States has changed dramatically. The basis of the nation's economy has shifted from farming to industry to technology. Through each of these transitions, the global population has continued to grow, increasing the need to produce more food more efficiently.

Food scientists have played a key role in scaling up production to meet this demand. They've harnessed technological breakthroughs to navigate cultural shifts and world events. Nowhere are the changes to the food system more apparent than in farming.

INDUSTRIALIZED FARMING

As the farming industry has worked to feed the world, government agencies have created incentives

The American Farm Bureau Federation predicts US farms
will need to produce 70 percent more food in 2050 than in
the 2020s to support the world's growing population.

for farmers to increase production. Farmers shifted from growing low-yield crops, such as rye, to higher-yield crops, such as wheat and barley. Machines also replaced animal labor on farms. This increased production and efficiency, but it also led to a decrease in available manure. With less of this natural fertilizer available, scientists worked to create a chemical alternative.

A method of producing nitrogen-based fertilizer was developed in the early 1900s by German chemists Fritz Haber and Carl Bosch. The process involved combining hydrogen from natural gas with nitrogen pulled from the atmosphere and placing the gases under high pressure. A metal, such as iron, was used as a catalyst, a substance that speeds up the chemical reaction.

THE GREEN REVOLUTION

The green revolution swept the world in the 1950s and 1960s. New machinery and innovations, such as modern irrigation systems, pesticides, synthetic fertilizers, high-yield crops, and hybrid crops, were developed to help feed a growing population. But monocropping has caused many indigenous crops to become extinct or endangered, including many varieties of sweet corn. A seed catalog published in 1903 included 307 options for sweet corn. Only 12 of these varieties exist today.[1] Pesticides and fertilizers also threaten an already overtaxed water supply. A new revolution may be underway as scientists look for ways to increase crop yields while limiting negative effects on the environment.

The hydrogen and nitrogen reacted to form ammonia gas, which was then condensed using cold water. The end result was a liquid ammonia called anhydrous ammonia that farmers could apply to their fields. Mass production of the fertilizer began after World War II in factories that had once produced ammonium nitrate for bombs.

Chemical fertilizers fueled the next wave of farming advancements as large farming enterprises began to buy out smaller farms in the mid-1950s. From 1950 to the 1990s, the total number of farms in the United States dropped from 5.39 million to 1.91 million.[2] The farms that remained tended to be large operations. They specialized in distinct crops, with a focus on profit and efficiency.

Instead of growing many crops, farms began to grow a single product, a practice known as monocropping. To meet the increased demand for production, farmers used pesticides, fertilizers, and extensive irrigation systems. They also sought out new plant varieties that produced more robust products with higher yields.

Food scientists developed genetically modified organisms (GMOs) for varieties of common crops, such as corn, soybeans, and sugar beets. Some GMOs are created through genetic engineering. This is a way to breed plants

Various groups, including the Non-GMO Project, have advocated for transparency in food labeling so that consumers know whether their food includes genetically modified ingredients.

to have certain characteristics by adjusting the plants' DNA. Scientists seek out plants that produce more food. For example, they may look for corn with bigger kernels or more cobs per plant. Then scientists insert the genes linked to those traits into the DNA of a variety of corn that resists disease. Scientists can also use genetic engineering to turn off genes for certain undesirable traits in plants.

The first genetically modified vegetables appeared in supermarket produce sections in 1994. Ten years later, 90 percent of the corn, soybeans, and cotton grown on US farms was genetically modified.[3] In addition to higher yields, these foods resist pests and disease, last longer on the shelf, and have a better taste.

INCREASED ANIMAL PRODUCTION

Science has played a role in increasing production in animals as well. Animals have been bred to grow bigger or produce more in a shorter amount of time. Modern broiler chickens were developed in 1948 during the Chicken of Tomorrow competition sponsored by the USDA. The challenge was to develop a stronger bird that had more meat.

The winning bird was raised by Charles Vantress of California, who bred a Cornish chicken with an East Coast broiler variety called New Hampshire. Vantress won the contest again three years later, and his hybrid chickens sired 60 percent of the broiler chickens bred in the United States. This hybrid has allowed farmers to raise chickens in half the time. In 1925, it took an average of 112 days for a broiler chicken to grow to 2.5 pounds (1.13 kg), the market weight. By 2019, it took only 47 days for broilers to reach a market weight of 6.32 pounds (2.87 kg). Critics argue that the birds are raised in tight quarters to quickly grow to a weight that is unhealthy. Some birds do not live longer than two months.[4]

Dairy cows have also been bred to produce more milk. Breeds such as Ayrshire, Brown Swiss, Guernsey, Holstein-Friesian, and Jersey make up the commercial dairy cow industry. In the early 1800s, a cow would produce less than 396 gallons (1,500 L), or 3,300 pounds (1,500 kg), of milk per year. In 2024, after extensive breeding, a cow can be expected to produce 1,717 gallons (6,500 L), or 14,300 pounds (6,500 kg), of milk each year.[5]

Tom Kestell, owner of Ever-Green-View Farm in Waldo, Wisconsin, has a cow that set a national record for milk production in 2017. His Holstein, My Gold, produced 77,480 pounds (35,140 kg) in a year, compared with the average 22,770 pounds (10,330 kg). Kestell chalks up the success of his cows to good breeding. He says, "Our goal is to take care of our cows, breed good cows, have good cows, sell good cows to other people, and then let the pieces fall where they may."[6]

Breeding dairy cattle once involved finding cows with desirable traits, such as producing milk with lots of butterfat or protein. These quality milk producers would then be bred with cows known for being strong and healthy. More selective breeding would take place in the following generations until a breed with the desired traits was created. Today, artificial insemination makes the process more efficient.

In 2009, the bovine genome was discovered. This made it possible to easily find breeds known for producing a

Geneticists mapped the bovine genome. This process showed scientists which genes were responsible for specific traits in cows.

lot of milk. The sperm of a bull from a line of cattle with desirable traits is injected into a young female for the first time at the age of 15 months. The cow is injected again three months after giving birth, as a cow must birth one calf per year to continue producing milk. Cows typically produce large amounts of milk for only three years.[7] After that time, cows at commercial dairy farms are sold and slaughtered for beef.

Livestock practices have also become industrialized. The majority of US meat products are raised in concentrated animal feeding operations (CAFOs). These are farms that have animals weighing one million pounds (450,000 kg) in total that are fed a lot of corn and soy, with the goal of taking the mature animals to market in a short amount of time.[8] Most poultry and pork products come from large facilities that produce more than 200,000 chickens or 5,000 pigs per year. Egg-laying hens are housed in vast barns with more than 100,000 other birds.[9]

NEW PROBLEMS TO SOLVE

These advancements have introduced new problems for food scientists to solve. Crowded housing and unsanitary conditions create health challenges for the animals. In close quarters, diseases can spread quickly, so some farmers give livestock regular doses of antibiotics to control infections.

Consumers and health advocates have expressed concerns about antibiotics in meat, milk, or eggs from treated animals. Some research has indicated that antibiotics in the food supply can have negative effects on human health, causing allergic reactions and issues with the kidneys, liver, and reproductive system. In response, the FDA now requires that animals be free of antibiotics for a certain length of time before they are slaughtered.

Other challenges include the effects that corporate livestock farms, chemical fertilizers, and chemical pesticides have on humans and the environment. The increasing number of corporate farms means more pollution. The Environmental Protection Agency (EPA) counted 20,300 corporate farms in 2018, nearly five times the number that existed 40 years before.[11] The vast amount of manure generated on these farms affects the air quality and pollutes nearby lakes, streams, and groundwater. The methane gas emitted by livestock is a greenhouse gas that contributes to climate change.

As US corporate farms cultivate more land, farmers are using more synthetic fertilizers. This is a major source of the increase in nitrous oxide, another greenhouse gas,

Regulatory organizations determine how much space farms must provide for animals. Chickens, for example, are afforded less than one square foot (0.09 sq m) each.

in the atmosphere. The use of synthetic pesticides has increased as well. These chemicals pollute streams, lakes, and groundwater. People who ingest them, whether through drinking contaminated water, breathing tainted air, or eating food grown with pesticides, face potential health issues. Pesticides have been found to contribute to the risk of cancer and may negatively affect the immune system, the nervous system, and the reproductive system.

INDUSTRIALIZED FOOD

In the United States, food is big business. In 2023, total retail and food service sales reached $8.33 trillion.[12] Processed foods made up most of the calories Americans consumed. Food manufacturers strive to produce foods efficiently and inexpensively while making a profit. They know that people's first consideration when comparing products is often taste, not nutrition. So manufacturers and food

Developed in 2009, the Yale Food Addiction Scale (YFAS) assesses symptoms of addiction-like eating, using the same criteria psychiatrists use to identify substance dependence. The scale considers 11 different categories, including craving specific foods, inability to stop eating, and withdrawal symptoms such as excessive irritability or anxiety.[14] Consumers experiencing addiction-like symptoms were most likely to eat UPFs high in refined carbohydrates and sugars, salt, and fats. Studies show that these foods create the same reaction in the brain as nicotine and alcohol.

scientists continue to look for ways to make products look and taste more appealing while keeping companies profitable and competitive. The solution is often to add an irresistible combination of sugar, fat, and salt to processed foods.

Sugar, fat, and salt are used in a variety of ways in industrial food processing. In moderation, sugar can be part of a healthy diet. However, the majority of sugar eaten by kids and adults today comes from processed foods. Each year the average American eats more than 70 pounds (32 kg) of sweeteners from sugar cane, sugar beets, and high-fructose corn syrup.[13] Added sugar improves the smell, appearance, and texture of foods.

Added fat makes chips crisp, softens bread, and prevents hot dogs from sticking to the pan. Fat prolongs shelf life and replaces water to make products more tender. Fat masks acidity and enhances aroma. Fat also contains twice as many calories as sugar. Salt, when combined with fat and sugar, adds flavor to foods, providing a cheap alternative to fresh herbs and spices. These ingredients, plus other additives and preservatives, add to the shelf life and profitability of the industrial food system.

Virtually every aspect of the food system is being re-evaluated. Critics of the current system argue that advancements and technology have outpaced our ability to develop guidelines and legislation to protect the food system. Food scientists have created solutions that sometimes cause as many problems as they've solved. However, the research food scientists conduct is key to developing and monitoring a sustainable food system that provides healthy food for a growing planet and protects the environment.

CHAPTER FIVE

THE IMPACTS OF THE FOOD SYSTEM

Consumers are becoming more aware of the social, environmental, and economic impacts of their food choices. Many people are concerned about the amount of fossil fuels used to transport goods around the world. They are also worried about food insecurity closer to home, as well as other issues related to the food system. Many consumers want to see positive change. Food scientists search for solutions that address these important challenges.

FOOD AND SOCIAL JUSTICE

Malnutrition and food insecurity continue to threaten many parts of the world, even though overall global food production remains high. In 2022, between 691 and 783 million people faced hunger. Another 3.1 billion people could not afford a healthy diet.[1] Though UPFs are more affordable,

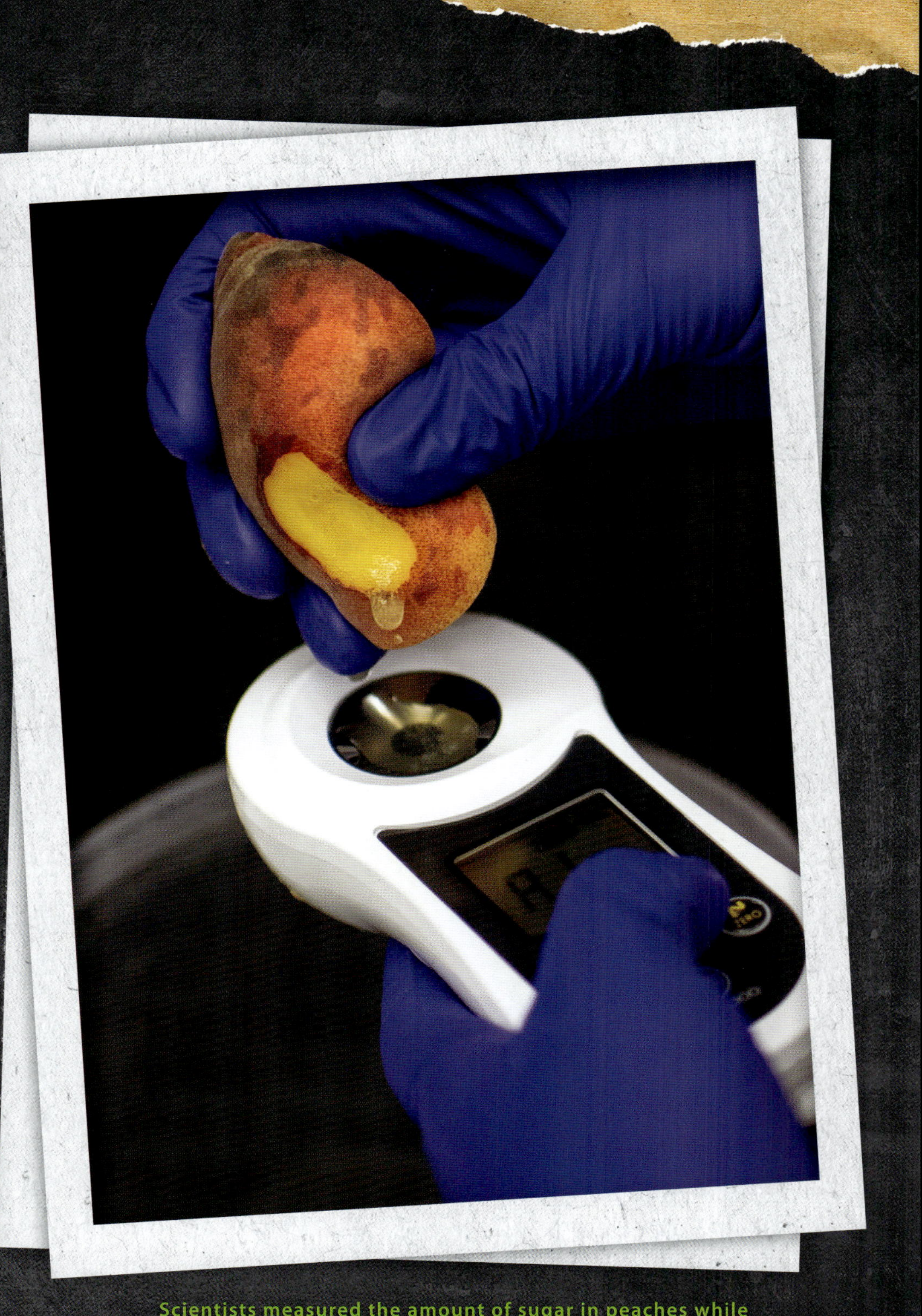

Scientists measured the amount of sugar in peaches while developing new methods to prevent ripening. This allows fruits to stay fresh longer while reducing food waste.

many experts believe that their low nutritional value and high caloric content have created more problems than they've solved.

In the United States, 12.8 percent of households struggle with food insecurity.[2] People belonging to racial and ethnic minorities and people of lower socioeconomic status are more likely to struggle with food insecurity. They tend to live in areas with fewer healthy sources for foods. People in these groups also have less disposable income to spend on foods with higher nutritional value. Instead, they must rely on fast food and cheap, high-calorie UPFs.

A diet heavy in UPFs can have serious health consequences for communities. Consuming too many UPFs has been linked to an increase in heart disease, stroke, diabetes, cancer, irritable bowel syndrome (IBS), depression, dementia, and asthma. In the United States, Black, Hispanic, and Asian American adults are more likely than white adults to develop type 2 diabetes, a disease in which there is too much sugar circulating in the blood. An unhealthy diet contributes to the development of this disease.

Meanwhile, in 2021, food and beverage companies spent 73 percent of their advertising budgets to promote candy, cereal, snacks, and sugary drink products on media outlets that are popular with Black people and Spanish speakers.[3] Deliberately targeting Black and Hispanic consumers for UPFs further contributes to the inequities.

FINDING SOLUTIONS

Social problems, including racially targeted marketing and food inequity, often require complex solutions that blend grassroots activism, science, government policy, and health education. Food scientists are trying to address these issues by increasing the nutritional value of food products. For example, they have developed pinto beans that retain more iron after cooking and pasta made from beans that contains more protein and minerals than traditional wheat pastas. Researchers have found ways to lower the glycemic index in rice while also raising the amount of protein. Glycemic index

Pasta made from chickpeas is a higher-protein, higher-fiber alternative to wheat pasta. However, chickpea pasta is often more expensive than traditional options.

is a measurement of how quickly a food can increase the level of sugar in a person's blood. This is important for those with diabetes.

Other food scientists are working to reduce the excess salt, sugar, and fat consumers crave in their favorite snack foods without sacrificing the taste, appearance, or texture. Gregory Ziegler teaches food science at Penn State University. He says, "Researchers are studying how we perceive sweetness and saltiness, and how we might modify either the composition or the structure of foods to deliver the best sweetness from the least amount of sugar."[4]

Scientists are working to alter sugar's structure so that it dissolves on the tongue more quickly, which they hope will lead people to desire less sugar in products. But altering a food's structure can affect the food's nutritional value. Scientists are working to produce healthier foods that still have an appealing taste.

FOOD AND THE ENVIRONMENT

The global food system must come up with innovative solutions to reduce its negative impact on the environment. The food system is estimated to be the largest single source of human-induced environmental harm, responsible for around a quarter of the world's greenhouse gas emissions. Seventy percent of the world's freshwater usage goes to agriculture,

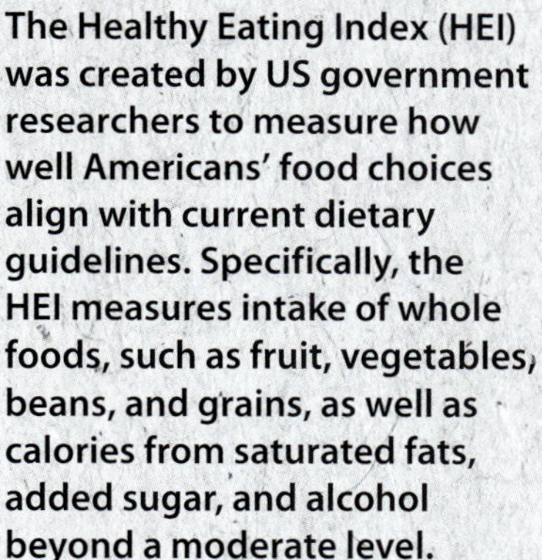

THE HEALTHY EATING INDEX (HEI)

The Healthy Eating Index (HEI) was created by US government researchers to measure how well Americans' food choices align with current dietary guidelines. Specifically, the HEI measures intake of whole foods, such as fruit, vegetables, beans, and grains, as well as calories from saturated fats, added sugar, and alcohol beyond a moderate level.

In 2020, the nation's HEI score was 58 out of 100.[5] According to the National Institutes of Health, scores greater than 80 indicate a good diet, while scores between 51 and 80 need improvement.[6] Following dietary guidelines reduces the risk of diet-related chronic diseases.

stressing local water systems.[7] Food manufacturing releases contaminated water, which can pollute rivers and lakes.

Agriculture uses half of the world's habitable land. This is land that was once covered with forests and wetlands, which helped slow climate change by removing carbon dioxide from the air, storing carbon in the trees and soil, and releasing oxygen. Use of wild lands for agriculture has also contributed to the reduction of biodiversity in the world's wildlife. Globally, 94 percent of nonhuman mammal biomass is now livestock, while only 6 percent is wild.[8]

Industrialized farms use pesticides and herbicides that kill many essential bugs and plants that, while considered undesirable for raising crops, are essential to their ecosystems. Nitrogen-based fertilizers created to feed crops end up in nearby waterways, where they cause algae blooms that deplete the water of oxygen, kill fish, and disrupt habitats. Monocropping depletes the soil of nutrients and kills the soil's natural microorganisms.

The challenge of reducing and even reversing decades of damage to the environment is enormous. Food scientists work in microbiology and agriculture to find solutions. One way researchers are improving the agricultural side of the food system is by improving soil diversity. The soil

microbiome is a complex web of living things, including fungi, insects, bacteria, and yeasts. A teaspoon of healthy soil contains hundreds of millions or even billions of beneficial microorganisms.

Healthy soil grows nutritious, resilient crops. However, practices such as monocropping and using synthetic pesticides and nitrogen fertilizers rob soil of essential diversity. Instead, scientists are testing the effects of using biofertilizers, including manure, compost, and algae, and biopesticides, such as canola oil or baking soda.

CONTROLLED ENVIRONMENT AGRICULTURE

Indoor farming may be the future of feeding the world. Controlled environment agriculture (CEA) is gaining momentum thanks to new sensor technologies, better LED lighting, and improved climate control systems. Growing food in greenhouses and indoor farms uses less water, pesticides, and fertilizer.

A wide range of produce can be grown and used locally throughout the year, regardless of the climate outdoors. CEA crops, including greens, tomatoes, and herbs, may be grown in soil, as they would be outdoors. Farmers may also grow them in nutrient-rich water in a process called hydroponics, or by hanging plants and misting the roots, called aeroponics.

These natural alternatives improve soil health. But runoff still needs to be managed, as even natural manure will pollute local waterways.

FOOD AND THE ECONOMY

Each year, diet-related diseases, including heart disease, stroke, and diabetes, are estimated to cost the United States $50 billion in health care expenses.[9] Food scientists can help lower the cost of diet-related health expenses by reformulating processed foods to include less added sugar. Sugar has been shown to be a major contributor to type 2 diabetes and is also highly addictive.

Food scientists also are using flavors to enhance a product's sweet taste without additional sugar. Flavors such as cinnamon and vanilla and some fruits can increase sweetness and mask the bitterness found in common replacement sweeteners, such as stevia or monk fruit. Using these flavors can reduce the added sugar in a food product without reducing the sweet flavor that consumers crave.

Food scientists also are working to improve the current food system. They are looking for solutions that address the social, environmental, and economic challenges inherent in how food is produced today. Together with other experts and researchers, they are creating a more sustainable and nutritious future, one innovation at a time.

CHAPTER SIX

FOOD SCIENCE INNOVATIONS

Two scientific solutions to particularly troubling issues in food—health and the environment—are as promising as they are complex and controversial. These are alternative proteins and GMOs. They offer new choices for consumers looking to improve their diet or help the environment. But these technologies are not without their risks and critics. Understanding the role of alternative proteins and GMOs in the food industry is crucial for navigating the diverse landscape of modern food choices.

ALTERNATIVE PROTEINS

Protein is found in animal products and in plants such as beans, legumes, and whole grains. A lack of adequate protein can lead to slowed growth in children, loss of muscle tissue, and anemia. In this

Debates about the use of GMOs have sparked protests around the world, many of which have called for mandatory labeling of genetically modified ingredients.

condition, a lack of iron causes blood cells to deliver less oxygen to the body than is needed.

Meat is the leading source of protein available in the United States. Up to 80 percent of American consumers prefer animal-sourced protein over plant-based proteins.[1] However, that number is shifting.

Animal products are an excellent source of not only protein but also vitamins and minerals, including zinc and iron. But animal products can also contain high amounts of saturated fat, which elevates blood cholesterol and increases the risk of heart disease. Diets high in red meat and processed meats, such as hot dogs and deli meats, have also been linked to bowel cancer.

Meat and dairy production account for 14.5 percent of global greenhouse gas emissions. The top four sources for emissions are beef, lamb

MORE ABOUT PROTEIN

The human body needs adequate protein to function. Protein provides energy, makes hormones and enzymes, and builds and repairs muscle and bone. Protein is a biomolecule, a combination of 20 different amino acids. The body makes 11 nonessential amino acids and gets the remaining essential amino acids through food. Dietary guidelines recommend at least 5.5 ounces (156 g) of protein each day. A three-ounce (85 g) serving of cooked meat is about the size of a deck of playing cards.[2]

and sheep, farmed shrimp, and dairy cows, with beef contributing more than twice as much carbon as lamb and sheep.[3] As consumers shift their diets and nations look to reduce their emissions, food scientists are developing several alternatives to animal-sourced proteins, including lab-grown or cultivated meat and plant-based meat. Each approach comes with drawbacks and advantages, but all share the goal of supplementing or replacing animal-sourced proteins.

CULTIVATED ANIMAL PRODUCTS

Perhaps the most complex and controversial alternative to animal-sourced proteins is cultivated meat, also known as lab-grown, clean, or cultured meat. Cultivated meat uses the food technology of cellular agriculture. This process involves using live animal cells to produce meat that is identical to the burgers, steaks, and chicken that consumers are used to eating.

Cultivated meat begins by taking a sample of tissue from a living animal. Stem cells from the sample are placed in a bioreactor or cultivator, which creates the ideal environment for cell growth. A medium containing salt, sugar, fat, and other substances that promote cell growth is added. This is everything the cells need to grow. Once the cells have

Cultivated meat is grown in large stainless-steel tanks. Depending on how it is prepared, lab-grown meat may look and taste similar to its traditional animal counterpart.

formed muscle tissue, scientists change the medium in the bioreactor two more times to grow fat and connective tissue, components needed to replicate the appearance and taste of traditional meat. Structural materials known as scaffolding are added as well, providing a surface for the cells to grow into a desired shape.

Animal-free dairy, also known as precision dairy, can be grown without the use of animal cells. This is done using the process of precision fermentation, which encodes microflora, or tiny organisms such as yeast and bacteria, with DNA from dairy proteins such as milk. These microflora are given nutrients and sugars to promote growth. As a result, the microflora produce casein and whey, the proteins found in milk. These products are made into animal-free milk, cream cheese, ice cream, egg whites, and chocolate. Animal-free dairy and eggs are being used in food products around the world. These products are identical to traditional dairy products.

Advocates of cultured meat and animal-free dairy say they provide ethical and sustainable alternatives to animal-sourced products. Each hour, 11 million land animals are slaughtered for food. Globally, 70 billion farm animals are being raised for food, often in crowded conditions.[4]

Raising livestock is also expensive and inefficient. For example, a single cow must be raised, housed, and fed for two years before it can yield 800 quarter-pound (0.11 kg) burger patties. In contrast, cultured meat uses a small sample of cells from one living cow to produce 80,000 of those patties in as little as five weeks.[5] Advocates also say that cultivated meat and precision dairy can be produced with fewer greenhouse gas emissions than traditional livestock.

Critics of cultured meat and animal-free dairy point out that these food products are novel to the human body. Researchers are still investigating their effects on human health. The industry hasn't been transparent about research findings, so claims regarding lower greenhouse gas emissions are difficult to verify. Currently, some lab-grown meat requires pharmaceutical-grade ingredients, which require large amounts of energy to process.

But other lab-grown meat is made with food-grade ingredients, which have lower energy needs and emissions. Scientists estimate that pharmaceutical lab-grown meat could be more expensive and have up to 25 times greater climate change impact than traditional meat.[6] Food-grade lab meat, however, would be slightly more energy efficient than the current US meat products. Scientists continue to research methods to make cultivated meat a truly sustainable alternative.

PLANT-BASED PROTEINS

Plant-based proteins have been available since the 1960s in restaurants and since the 1980s in supermarkets. Early plant-based meats were created for vegetarians and vegans who wanted to replace animal-based proteins with plant-based alternatives. These early products didn't try to mimic the look and feel of conventional meat. In recent decades, new techniques and technology, along with higher mainstream consumer demand, have brought to the market more plant-based meat options that resemble animal proteins.

Animals and plants may not appear to share many similarities. But at a biochemical level, plants and animals are made of protein, fat, water, vitamins, and minerals. Developers re-create the nutritional content of meat and dairy by extracting those elements from plants and mimicking the texture and taste through chemical, mechanical, or biological processing.

Plant-based meat options are expanding to include meat-free replacements for steak, sausages, burger patties, chicken nuggets, fish sticks, meatballs, and more.

Coconuts, cashews, oats, almonds, and soybeans have been used to mimic milk, cheese, yogurt, and eggs. So far, producers of plant-based meats have had the most success using plants to form patties that mimic the texture of ground meats such as burgers. But food scientists around the world are developing new ways to produce whole cuts of plant-based meat, including steaks or chicken breasts.

United Kingdom–based Adamo Foods is creating steaks by fermenting mycelium, the rootlike part of a fungus that connects a community of mushrooms through an underground network. The structure of mycelium mimics

ANIMAL-FREE DAIRY

Cultivated meat is coming, but animal-free dairy is already here. Major food manufacturers Nestlé, Mars, and General Mills are using precision dairy in their products. Yogurt, cheese, chocolate, and ice cream made with animal-free dairy can now be purchased in stores across the United States. Even the coffee chain Starbucks began offering animal-free milk on a trial basis in Seattle, Washington, locations in 2021. Animal-free dairy can be made without cholesterol, lactose, growth hormones, or antibiotics, which could make it a healthier alternative. Whether consumers will widely accept this lab-grown dairy remains to be seen.

the tender yet sinewy texture of beef, provides nutritional benefits such as protein, fiber, and all nine essential amino acids, and is easier for people to digest than beef and many plant fibers. To create the steaks, developers grow slabs of mycelium inside a bioreactor and then ferment them.

Nick Wood, chief operating officer of Adamo Foods, explained this process: "We brew it in large bioreactors similar to how you brew beer. We fill a large fermenting vessel with a source of carbon, nitrogen, and some nutrients, inoculate it, and then we grow it over several days."[7] Then the slab is removed from the bioreactor, dried, and sliced into steaks. Developers are also looking for ways to fortify the mycelium with omega-3 fatty acids during the fermentation stage. Omega-3 fatty acids support heart and lung functions, the immune system, and the endocrine system, which produces and balances hormones.

Proponents of plant-based technology say that eating more foods made with plants can reduce greenhouse gas emissions while improving human health. But consumers have been slow to shift to plant-based meats, which made up only about 1 percent of the food retail market in the United States in 2023.[8] Consumers have more widely accepted plant-based milk, which accounts for around 15 percent of the retail milk market.[9]

Others wonder about the health benefits of products that, though derived from plants, are as far from their natural state as other ultra-processed foods on the market. And consumers continue to find the taste and texture of many plant-based foods lacking. For plant-based foods to take off, experts say the industry needs more resources. This includes more financial investment, more scientists, new research, and new technology.

GMOs

Humans have created hybrid plants and animals for centuries to produce desirable traits through selective breeding and cross breeding, or hybridization. For example,

Scientists may test several iterations of a GMO to ensure that the desired trait is expressed and the food is safe to consume.

dogs can be bred for friendliness by selectively breeding only the friendliest dogs. Strawberries sold in markets today are a hybrid of two species that, when combined, create a variety capable of producing larger fruit. However, breeding can take many generations and produce inconsistent results. To develop GMOs, scientists change the DNA of an organism to create a new variety with the desired traits in a single generation.

To produce a GMO, scientists identify a trait or traits that are desirable for an organism, such as pest resistance in corn or faster growth in salmon. They then find a second organism, which could be a plant, animal, or microorganism, with those traits they are looking for. Scientists locate and copy the genes responsible for those traits and insert them into the DNA of the first organism. Once the new organism is grown, it's tested for the desired trait.

If the modification has been successful, the developer can apply for FDA approval to sell the new organism to farmers. For example, scientists looking to reduce the amount of pesticide used in growing corn isolated a gene in a soil bacteria that was used as a natural insecticide. They then inserted that gene into corn to improve the corn's resistance to insect damage.

Approximately 90 percent of the corn, soybeans, and sugar beets grown today are GMOs.[10] These plants are bred for high yields, long shelf life, and resistance to pests and herbicides. GMO technology has also been applied to animals, although the majority of these animals are used in research. A species of genetically modified salmon is now available in food markets.

THE FLAVR SAVR

In 1994, the first GMO to be sold in supermarkets reached store shelves. The Flavr Savr tomato looked like any other tomato. However, the Flavr Savr had a longer shelf life than its counterparts because it was genetically modified to deactivate the gene responsible for fruit softening. Consumers widely accepted the new tomatoes, which were approved for sale in the United States by the FDA. Today, many genetically engineered plants and animals are available, including a plum-colored tomato that was combined with a snapdragon flower for color.

This salmon has been genetically engineered to continually produce growth hormones so that it matures faster, which reduces the time and expense of raising it.

Advocates of genetically engineered crops say farmers can grow more crops faster, increasing their profits while reducing the use of water, pesticides, and fertilizers. Critics worry that wide use of GMOs could reduce plant and animal diversity. Diversity is necessary to help plants fight diseases and protect plant species against climate change. A variety of species means plants have a broader genetic makeup, allowing them to better adapt to these threats.

But genetically engineered crops have also allowed some farmers to avoid disaster. In the 1990s, ringspot virus disease devastated Hawaii's papaya crop, nearly driving the Hawaiian papaya industry to extinction. Scientists responded with the GMO Rainbow papaya, which resisted ringspot virus and allowed Hawaiian papaya farmers to recover. By 2016, 90 percent of papayas grown in Hawaii were Rainbow papayas.[11]

Critics point out that GMOs that have been developed to resist damage from herbicides, which are used to kill weeds in crop fields, have actually led to an increase in herbicide use and the emergence of herbicide-resistant superweeds.

This happens when weeds containing genes that resist the herbicide reproduce with a crop plant that has been genetically engineered. Since the introduction of GMOs in the United States, the use of the herbicide glyphosate, which is believed to cause cancer in humans, has increased by 16 times.[12] Overuse of herbicides has also led to a decline in native plants.

Another challenge is that GMOs are patented intellectual property owned by a few large corporations with restrictive license agreements. That means that each year farmers must purchase new seeds from these corporations instead of harvesting seeds from the previous year's plants. Critics worry about the impact of large, for-profit organizations holding too much control over agriculture and the global food supply.

Meat and dairy alternatives as well as GMOs have the potential to help the food system keep pace with a growing world population. However, these technologies may also come with downsides. Research into and debate over their impact on the environment and human health will continue to shape the food industry's future.

CHAPTER SEVEN

CAREERS IN FOOD SCIENCE

areers in food science offer an enticing blend of creative and scientific exploration. Food scientists are at the forefront of inventing new flavors, upholding food safety standards, and revolutionizing food packaging to minimize waste. From crafting the perfect chocolate bar to developing sustainable agricultural practices for a healthier planet, a career in food science offers many exciting opportunities. Future food scientists may even help feed astronauts on their way to Mars.

FOOD TECHNOLOGIST

Food technologists make sure new food products meet all the rules. They may study food science, agriculture, microbiology, biochemistry, or chemistry. Food technologists often work closely with food manufacturers and government agencies.

Food scientists may spend time in a laboratory conducting research on new food products.

They may spend their days in labs, crafting new ideas, or work on-site in manufacturing plants, overseeing production and testing.

Food technologists are responsible for the safety and quality of food products. They ensure the foods are produced safely and within regulatory guidelines. Food technologists may also invent new recipes and techniques, source ingredients to improve products, or find ways to package and preserve foods to maintain taste and nutritional value. Depending on their roles, food technologists may work with scientific research equipment in labs or use standard refrigerators, blenders, and ovens in a kitchen.

FOOD MICROBIOLOGIST

Food microbiologists often work on the front lines of the food industry to ensure the safety of the food system. They analyze the microorganisms in food and study how they can affect human health and food selection.

Food microbiologists study microbial physiology, genetics, virology, and food safety. They may work in research and quality control labs, directly with manufacturers, or with government and regulatory agencies. They may also find ways to fortify foods with healthy bacteria, or they may work with microorganisms involved in fermentation.

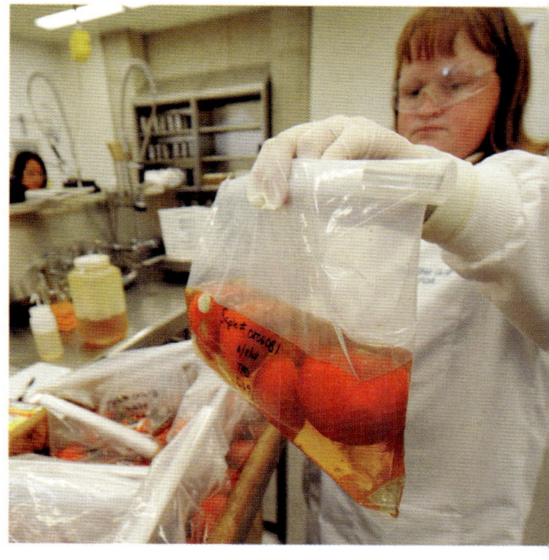

Food microbiologists help health agencies track the source of food poisoning outbreaks by testing various suspected foods.

Food microbiologists may analyze samples of food products for contamination by microorganisms that cause foodborne illnesses, such as *Salmonella* or *Listeria*. They research food to understand why it becomes contaminated so they can prevent it from happening in the future. They may also study how microbes affect the shelf life of a food product, and they can educate consumers on safe food handling and storage techniques.

Food microbiologists ensure that food products meet government safety and health regulations and work to establish new food safety standards. They also use microorganisms such as yeast in crafting food products, including bread and yogurt. Understanding these microorganisms helps food microbiologists create tastier, healthier, and safer food products.

FLAVOR CHEMIST

Flavor chemists, or flavorists, are the tastemakers of the food industry. Their work is part science, part art. Working with approved natural and synthetic flavors and extracts, flavorists develop new flavor profiles for food and beverage products that will appeal to consumers. A flavor profile is the combination of tastes, aromas, and textures that make up the overall taste of a recipe. Flavorists may study food science and chemistry and undergo a rigorous apprenticeship with a flavor company before working as a food chemist.

The flavors created by chemists help mask undesirable aspects of food, including bitterness or sourness. Flavors can also enhance a taste that's desirable. Part of creating new flavors is understanding how processing, such as cooking, affects a product's flavor and aroma. Process and reaction flavor chemists mimic or enhance the taste, aroma, and texture of cooked foods using sugars, amino acids, and fats.

Because they are considered ingredient manufacturers, flavorists closely follow FDA and USDA regulations regarding food additives. Flavorists' creations are used widely in today's foods, with more than 90 percent of foods in grocery stores containing added flavors.[2]

SENSORY SCIENTIST

Sensory scientists study how to make food more appealing to consumers. Sensory scientist Anna Chow Fry is often asked about her job. She says, "To put it in simpler terms, it's obtaining people's reactions to products in terms of how it smells, tastes, looks, feels, and sounds and then using this information to make decisions. Whenever there is a question about product differences and likes or dislikes, sensory [science] is usually involved. It's a mixture of food

BECOME A PROFESSIONAL FOOD TASTER

Once sensory scientists have created a new product, they rely on human response to tell them whether consumers will buy it in stores. To do this, they set up a taste testing session with a panel of food tasters, who may be volunteers or professionals. Professional food tasters have a strong sense of taste and can distinguish layers of flavors. They are also able to communicate what they're tasting clearly to researchers. Tasters undergo in-depth palate training that creates sensory memory, helping them identify traits and ingredients in foods.

Sensory scientists may ask the general public to taste foods. One experimenter played different types of music while cheeses aged, then asked the public about their tastes.

science, psychology, statistics, and consumer insights all rolled into one."[3]

Sensory scientists work with tasters who are trained to detect the presence of certain sensory elements in food groups. These elements include tastes, aromas, and textures. A sensory scientist may work with food manufacturers to create a new product or test whether consumers can taste changes in an existing product's ingredients. They help evaluate and analyze the results from sensory testing and adjust recipes and ingredients to make them more appealing. This may involve changing ingredients or improving the processing. Sensory scientists also help food manufacturers evaluate their products to make them more competitive and profitable.

SPACE FOOD SCIENTIST

Space food scientists support human space exploration by providing nutritious, safe, and shelf-stable food to astronauts. In the United States, space food scientists work for the National Aeronautics and Space Administration (NASA). NASA space food scientists may study nutrition and food science, safety, engineering, and processing. Their current work is to provide food for astronauts on missions to the International Space Station. They will also provide food for Artemis missions to the moon and eventually for deep space missions to Mars.

Space food scientists work with unique challenges. The food they create must be accessible to astronauts who are living in a microgravity environment for extended periods of time. Space food provides critical nutrition that can improve mental well-being for astronauts, who can spend months away from home at a time. The products that space food scientists test may last for up to five years.[4] These ready-to-eat meals are preserved through thermostabilization or freeze-drying. Space food scientists also repackage some of the astronauts' favorite store-bought foods so astronauts can enjoy the taste of home.

NUTRITIONIST

Nutritionists explore how food and the food system affect human health and well-being. They study chemistry, biology, genetics, and microbiology, along with human development, nutrition, and health. Nutritionists may work with government agencies to establish new labeling standards or dietary guidelines. They also work in labs, manufacturing plants, and offices where they create foods that meet special requirements for consumers with allergies or food sensitivities.

Nutrition is the foundation for a healthier life, so nutritionists often advise and educate a variety of health professionals on treating chronic diseases through diet.

They consult with public health officials to develop programming, guidelines, and initiatives to improve the eating habits of a population. They may also research the impact of certain foods, such as UPFs, on health and advise the industry on ways to improve the quality of the food supply.

Careers in food science appeal to a variety of scientific and creative interests. Food scientists are passionate about developing exciting new flavors, ensuring food safety, and keeping the food system safe and sustainable. From the lab to the farm, food scientists play a vital role in shaping the future of the food industry and the planet.

PERIODIC TABLE OF FOOD INITIATIVE

Food scientists are part of a global effort to develop new dietary guidelines that are environmentally sustainable. The Periodic Table of Food Initiative is a wide-reaching public database that aims to answer questions such as these: What is in the foods people eat? How do climate, location, and food production processes affect food quality? And how do these differences in food quality affect people and the Earth? Food scientists are gathering data about foods using mass spectrometry technologies, a process that identifies and characterizes proteins. The database will help scientists find sustainable farming practices that produce nutrient-dense foods, improve food quality, and clarify what makes up a healthy diet.

CHAPTER EIGHT

THE FUTURE OF FOOD SCIENCE

The future of food science is incredibly exciting. New technologies are revolutionizing the way we think about and create food. Chefs are using science to understand how different ingredients interact to create amazing flavors and textures. Consumers can print out their favorite snacks in 3D, such as instant pies and tasty cakes. With gene editing, scientists are making fruits and vegetables healthier and tastier than ever before. These advancements and others are changing not only how people eat but also how people think about food.

MOLECULAR GASTRONOMY

French physical chemist Hervé This has turned the art of cooking into a precise science called molecular gastronomy, which is a form of food preparation that relies on scientific techniques. One type of molecular

Futuristic foods, including those prepared using molecular
gastronomy, may not look like traditional meals. Chef
Gaggan Anand prepares a dish that resembles a painting.

gastronomy is note-by-note cooking. The chemist believes that note-by-note cooking can end world hunger by reducing spoilage and preserving essential compounds and nutrients of foods. To do this, chefs remove any moisture from the food and use only the food's most essential elements, nutrients, and flavors.

Using different techniques, these compounds are converted into powders, liquids, foams, and gels that are far easier to ship than traditional meats and vegetables. One technique is adding carbon dioxide to pureed foods to form foam. Others include freezing foods with liquid nitrogen or adding maltodextrin to convert fatty foods, such as bacon, into a powder. Many of these foods can be preserved nearly indefinitely.

Note-by-note cooking is often compared to composing a piece of music,

FOOD NEOPHOBIA

Neophobia is the fear of new or novel things. In the food industry, neophobia can prevent consumers from accepting a new product or adapting to changes in familiar foods, even if those changes are better for their health or the environment. Humans have psychological and emotional responses to foods, which are often at the center of community events and time-honored traditions. Food scientists look for ways to tie new foods and ideas to familiar ones, hoping to ease the path for technologies, such as 3D printed meat, that might otherwise meet resistance.

where each sound is added note by note. Hervé This
envisions a world where chefs and home cooks re-create a
host of culinary delights not by using meat and vegetables
and grains but by combining the compounds responsible for
their taste, texture, and nutrients.

Cooking with molecular compounds also has
the potential to be far more energy efficient and
environmentally sound because it requires fewer natural
resources for shipping or refrigeration and reduces food
waste and spoilage. Molecular gastronomy is used mostly
by scientists and highly trained chefs, but molecular
gastronomists hope their methods will one day be embraced
by home cooks too. So far, consumers haven't taken to the
idea of eating pillowy meat clouds or fish proteins in gel
form. As the world population grows, however, and humans
explore deeper into space, note-by-note cooking could play
a wider role in feeding the world.

CRISPR, GENETIC SCISSORS

Clustered regularly interspaced short palindromic repeats
(CRISPR) are parts of the DNA sequences of bacteria. They
help to chop up the DNA of invading viruses, making them
harmless. Often called genetic scissors, CRISPR can be

Scientists are using CRISPR gene editing to test new ways of growing plants in space.

used as a powerful genome editing tool. Scientists have used it to edit, or cut, a targeted sequence of DNA in animals, plants, and microorganisms. In food applications, CRISPR gene editing is simpler, cheaper, and more precise than other methods of genetic modification. CRISPR also has more uses.

In agriculture, CRISPR-edited chickens are being grown to resist avian flu and cancer-causing viruses. With the use of CRISPR, tomatoes grow bigger and have more vitamin D, mushrooms brown more slowly once sliced, and it's possible to grow wheat that doesn't trigger a reaction in people who have gluten sensitivities. In the chocolate industry, CRISPR-edited cocoa trees, which provide the material to make chocolate, resist diseases that destroy up to 30 percent of the world's harvest each year.[1]

In food processing and production, researchers are exploring how CRISPR can be used to modify microorganisms involved in food fermentation processes. These include yeast and bacteria. The edited microorganisms can be used to improve the flavor, texture, and nutritional content of fermented foods such as cheese, yogurt, and bread.

Though the potential uses for CRISPR in the future are exciting, many questions remain. One concern is the possible unintended consequences. For instance, producing chickens that resist avian flu could force viruses to mutate and spread more easily to mammals, including humans. Though CRISPR could help the world's crops adapt to the challenges of climate change, many people argue that this powerful technology needs to be carefully regulated to ensure it's being used safely and ethically.

FOOD AS MEDICINE

Neutraceuticals take the health benefits of natural foods and concentrate them into a pharmaceutical form, such as dietary supplements and vitamins. Neutraceuticals are used under the supervision of a doctor to treat diet-related diseases. They are also used in food manufacturing to fortify cereals and beverages with concentrated bioactive compounds. These are substances made of two or more different elements that have an effect on a living organism, tissue, or cell. Currently, neutraceuticals are poorly regulated and evaluated but are generally considered safer than chemical treatments. In the future, neutraceuticals could play a bigger role in treating diet-related diseases.

NEMO'S GARDEN: UNDERWATER FARMING

Underwater farming may sound like a fantasy, but off the coast of Noli, Italy, food scientists are putting it into practice. Nemo's Garden is an underwater farm composed of nine air-filled biospheres, or contained ecosystems, anchored to the seafloor. They are 15 to 36 feet (4.6–11 m) below the surface.[2] The goal of Nemo's Garden is to make underwater gardening an economically viable and eco-friendly option for meeting future food needs.

Nemo's Garden makes use of untapped space in the ocean. While only 11 percent of the world is arable land, or land that is suitable for growing crops, 70 percent of the planet's surface is covered by the ocean.[3] The pods also use renewable solar energy and desalinated ocean water to create a self-sustaining system. Each pod holds approximately 90 plants, including strawberries, green peas, herbs, and salad greens and also grows mushrooms.[4]

Inside the pods, humidity, light, temperature, carbon dioxide levels, and oxygen levels are monitored and carefully maintained remotely from land to ensure the plants' health, but no pesticides are needed.

Questions remain about whether underwater farming could be the future of food. Building a structure underwater and protecting it from saltwater corrosion and tropical storms can be difficult and costly. Much like greenhouses on land, underwater farms have high start-up costs. They also require trained scuba divers to access the harvest. Underwater gardening is still a small-scale solution to the problems in agriculture but has big potential to make a difference. In 2023, Nemo's Garden held more than 786 plants.[6] Its creators had plans to test cold-water biospheres in the United States.

3D PRINTED PIZZAS?

Since the mid-1980s, consumers and manufacturers have been exploring uses for 3D printers. These printers create three-dimensional objects by depositing layer after layer of a material such as plastic or metal. These printers have been used to make customized prosthetics, machine parts, medical implants, and housewares. Now, 3D printers in restaurants are printing foods using seafood puree and powdered onion. Manufacturers are developing 3D printed, plant-based fish filets and cultivated Japanese Wagyu steaks.

Food can be 3D printed using several methods. Extrusion is the most popular method. A printer forces pastes,

Foods that can be melted and then hardened, such as chocolate, may be printed using extrusion.

powders, and purees through a nozzle to form layers that build a 3D-shaped food, such as pizza dough or chocolate bars. Binder jetting is another method, commonly used with sugar. Water is injected into a powder to form a substance that hardens before the next layer is added.

At the moment, 3D printing food is mostly a novelty used to create foods in intricate and fun shapes and designs. Any printed food is highly processed. However, the technology is advancing, and scientists are researching a wide range of uses across the food system. Future soldiers may wear sensors connected to 3D printers that monitor their health and print on-demand rations that have been customized to meet their physical and nutritional needs. NASA is

TECHNOLOGY IN FOOD

The food industry is turning to technology to make the entire food system more efficient, profitable, and sustainable. In 2019, food tech was worth $220.32 billion globally.[7] Smart farms use automated machinery. Digital sensors and drones monitor crop health. Artificial intelligence (AI) predicts weather patterns. Robots are helping prepare and deliver food in restaurants, where smart appliances and software are helping owners minimize waste. In manufacturing, the use of robots is rising, bringing improvements to factory worker safety. The use of evolving technology in the food system will change the role of human workers, but it is also an essential tool in feeding a growing population.

working with corporations to develop a 3D printer to feed astronauts on their way to Mars. Experts predict that as the price for printers decreases and the need for convenience food increases, 3D printers will be as common in household kitchens as microwave ovens.

Food scientists face significant challenges in creating a healthy and sustainable food system. With the world's population steadily increasing and the prevalence of poor-quality ultra-processed foods contributing to diet-related diseases, change is needed. But the future of food science is bright. Future food scientists will play a pivotal role in developing innovative solutions. Whether it's through creating healthier food options, implementing sustainable agricultural practices, or advocating for policies that promote food equity, food scientists make a difference.

KIKUNAE IKEDA

While eating seaweed soup, Japanese chemist Kikunae Ikeda noticed a taste that didn't fit the basic four flavors—sweet, salty, bitter, and sour. He observed a similar flavor in other foods, such as tomato paste, cheese, and meat. Ikeda found that the amino acid glutamate was responsible for a fifth basic flavor, which he named "umami." Umami is described as a subtle but delectable taste that spreads across the tongue, lingers in the mouth, and promotes salivation. Ikeda also synthesized and patented monosodium glutamate, or MSG, as a food additive to create an umami-like taste.

MSG soon spread widely around the world. However, in the 1960s, public opinion and a few studies linked MSG to what was being called "Chinese Restaurant Syndrome." This involved headaches, dizziness, and other symptoms after eating Chinese food seasoned with MSG. The studies were limited and flawed, and much of the evidence was anecdotal and based in racism. But the damage was done.

The public began to avoid MSG. Today, MSG is making a comeback as the food industry looks to enhance umami elements in foods while reducing salt. MSG contains a fraction of the sodium in salt and is recognized as generally safe by the FDA.

FOOD SCIENCE BASICS

- Humans have been processing and preserving food for centuries. A growing world population, technological advances, and cultural shifts gave rise to the need for a scientific approach.

- Food scientists help make food safe, nutritious, appealing, and convenient for consumers.

- Natural and synthetic additives help preserve and improve food products that need a longer shelf life.

- The industrialized food system is a large contributor to the world's greenhouse gas emissions, leading food scientists to look for more sustainable methods to feed the global population.

FOOD SCIENCE SAFETY

- Experts have questioned the safety of many food additives because of negative effects on consumers' health.

- Food microbiologists study the microbes that cause foodborne illnesses and nonharmful food spoilage.

- Food processing allows food products to be safely shipped around the world and extends products' shelf lives.

- Government regulations and agencies such as the FDA protect consumers and provide oversight for the food industry.

THE RISE OF PROCESSED FOODS

- Processed foods are categorized into four main groups: unprocessed, processed culinary ingredients, processed, and ultra-processed foods (UPFs).

- UPFs have been linked to diabetes and other related diseases in consumers.

THE FUTURE OF FOOD SCIENCE

- Food scientists are developing protein alternatives to help feed a growing population and improve the environmental sustainability of the food system.

- From the lab to the farm to space, food scientists play a vital role in shaping the future of the food industry and the planet.

- Advances in food science include 3D printing of food, cooking with molecular compounds, and underwater farming.

QUOTE

"Whenever there is a question about product differences and likes or dislikes, sensory [science] is usually involved. It's a mixture of food science, psychology, statistics, and consumer insights all rolled into one."

—*Anna Chow Fry, sensory scientist*

additive
A chemical added to food during processing to create a desired result, such as added flavoring, stabilization of ingredients, or preservation.

biomass
The total mass of all the organisms in a given area.

contaminate
To make something impure, polluted, or potentially toxic.

crop yield
The amount of a crop, such as corn or wheat, harvested from an area of land during a single growing season.

fermentation
A metabolic process that produces chemical changes in organic substances through enzymes.

food grade
Describing a substance that can safely come into contact with food.

genome
An organism's complete set of genetic material.

greenhouse gas
One of several gases in the atmosphere that trap the sun's heat, leading to climate change.

irrigation
A system that brings water from one location to an area that has crops.

microbe
A microorganism, such as a bacterium, virus, or fungus.

microbiology
The study of microorganisms.

microorganism
A living thing too small to be seen with the naked eye.

patented
Recognized as the exclusive work of one person or group.

pharmaceutical grade
Approved for consumption by humans or animals by meeting strict purity standards.

polysaccharide
The most abundant carbohydrate found in food, consisting of bonded sugar molecules.

spoilage
The process of decay or decomposition in food, making the food inedible or undesirable to consumers.

stem cell
A basic cell with the potential to develop into many different types of cells in the body.

synthetic
Produced in a lab using chemicals.

toxic
Poisonous or harmful when consumed.

SELECTED BIBLIOGRAPHY

Delheimer, Sara. "Scientists across the Country Working to Create More Nutrient-Dense Diets." *National Institute of Food and Agriculture*, 7 Sept. 2023, nifa.usda.gov. Accessed 29 May 2024.

Miller, Korin. "What Are Ultra-Processed Foods, and Why Are They So Bad for You? Experts Explain." *Prevention*, 7 Feb. 2023, prevention.com. Accessed 18 June 2024.

"Understanding Food Nutrition Labels." *American Heart Association*, 3 Aug. 2023, heart.org. Accessed 22 Apr. 2024.

FURTHER READINGS

Allman, Toney. *The Future of Food: New Ideas about Eating*. ReferencePoint, 2021.

Lim, Angela. *The Crop Encyclopedia*. Abdo, 2024.

Wheeler, Jill C. *Modern Farming*. Abdo, 2025.

ONLINE RESOURCES

To learn more about food science, please visit **abdobooklinks.com** or scan this QR code. These links are routinely monitored and updated to provide the most current information available.

MORE INFORMATION

For more information on this subject, contact or visit the
following organizations:

NATIONAL INSTITUTE OF FOOD AND AGRICULTURE (NIFA)
12th St. SW and Jefferson Dr.
Washington, DC 20250
nifa.usda.gov

An agency of the US Department of Agriculture (USDA), the NIFA was
established to find innovative solutions to issues related to agriculture,
food, the environment, and communities.

SCIENCE HISTORY INSTITUTE
315 Chestnut St.
Philadelphia, PA 19106
sciencehistory.org

Founded in 1982, the Science History Institute is dedicated to
highlighting the hidden stories of the people responsible for significant
scientific achievements through research, storytelling, public
programming, and educational outreach.

SOCIETY OF FLAVOR CHEMISTS
3301 NJ-66, Ste. 220, Bldg. C
Neptune Township, NJ 07753
flavorchemists.com

Founded in 1954, the Society of Flavor Chemists is a not-for-profit
organization that advances the field of flavor creation and technology
and provides support and community for flavor chemists.

CHAPTER 1. THE WORLD OF FOOD SCIENCE

1. Autumn Swiers. "Why You Should Avoid the First Product on the Grocery Store Shelf." *Tasting Table*, 15 Sept. 2023, tastingtable.com. Accessed 5 Aug. 2024.

2. "Future of Food." *American Museum of Natural History*, n.d., amnh.org. Accessed 5 Aug. 2024.

3. Kat Eschner. "The Father of Canning Knew His Process Worked, but Not Why It Worked." *Smithsonian Magazine*, 2 Feb. 2017, smithsonianmag.com. Accessed 5 Aug. 2024.

4. Lizzie Wade. "How Egyptian Mummies Took Food to the Afterlife." *Wired*, 19 Nov. 2013, wired.com. Accessed 5 Aug. 2024.

5. James P. Sterba. "The History of Botulism." *New York Times*, 28 Apr. 1982, nytimes.com. Accessed 5 Aug. 2024.

6. Anna Zeide. "The Botulism Outbreak That Gave Rise to America's Food Safety System." *Smithsonian Magazine*, 3 Aug. 2018, smithsonianmag.com. Accessed 5 Aug. 2024.

7. Maria Godoy. "What We Know about the Health Risks of Ultra-Processed Foods." *NPR*, 25 May 2023, npr.org. Accessed 5 Aug. 2024.

CHAPTER 2. FOOD PROCESSING METHODS

1. "What's in a Name?—HPP vs. Pasteurization vs. Pascalization." *Universal Pure*, 12 Mar. 2020, universalpure.com. Accessed 5 Aug. 2024.

2. "What Is HPP Technology: The Solution to Achieve a Fresh, Safe and Minimally Processed Product." *Hiperbaric*, n.d., hiperbaric.com. Accessed 5 Aug. 2024.

3. "Foodborne Illnesses and Outbreaks." *California Department of Public Health*, 5 July 2024, cdph.ca.gov. Accessed 5 Aug. 2024.

4. Rebecca Jaspan. "These Are the Top 10 Foods Most Likely to Be Linked to Recalls and Disease Outbreaks." *Health*, 6 Apr. 2023, health.com. Accessed 5 Aug. 2024.

5. Emilie Le Beau Lucchesi. "This Hallucinogenic Fungus Might Be behind the Salem Witch Trials." *Discover Magazine*, 12 Oct. 2021, discovermagazine.com. Accessed 5 Aug. 2024.

CHAPTER 3. FOOD CHEMISTRY

1. Caroline Pullen. "Xanthan Gum—Is This Food Additive Healthy or Harmful?" *Healthline*, 3 Feb. 2023, healthline.com. Accessed 5 Aug. 2023.

2. "Buyer Beware: 60% of Foods Purchased by Americans Contain Technical Food Additives—a 10% Increase Since 2001." *Journal of the Academy of Nutrition and Dietetics*, 13 Mar. 2023, eatrightpro.org. Accessed 5 Aug. 2023.

3. Leonardo Trasande, MD, et al. "Food Additives and Child Health." *Pediatrics*, vol. 142, no. 2, 2018, *American Academy of Pediatrics*, publications.aap.org. Accessed 5 Aug. 2024.

4. Cara Murez. "More Additives Being Added to Americans' Food, Report Finds." *US News*, 15 Mar. 2023, usnews.com. Accessed 5 Aug. 2024.

5. Trasande et al., "Food Additives."

CHAPTER 4. THE INDUSTRIALIZED FOOD SYSTEM

1. Liz Scheltens. "The Race to Save Endangered Foods." *Vox*, 4 June 2019, vox.com. Accessed 5 Aug. 2024.

2 "Industrialization of Agriculture." *Johns Hopkins Center for a Livable Future*, n.d., foodsystemprimer.org. Accessed 5 Aug. 2024.

3. Julia M. Diaz and Judith L. Fridovich-Keil. "Genetically Modified Organism." *Encyclopedia Britannica*, 24 July 2024, britannica.com. Accessed 5 Aug. 2024.

4. Jennifer Mishler. "Outgrowing the Chicken House: A Brief History of the Modern Broiler Industry." *Sentient Food*, 16 Oct. 2020, sentientmedia.org. Accessed 5 Aug. 2024.

5. "Dairy Cattle Breeds." *Encyclopedia Britannica*, 10 May 2024, britannica.com. Accessed 20 June 2024.

6. Bridgit Bowden. "How We Produce More Milk with Fewer Cows." *Wisconsin Public Radio*, 28 Mar. 2017, wpr.org. Accessed 20 June 2024.

7. "Farm Animals: Dairy Cows." *Compassion in World Farming*, n.d., ciwf.org. Accessed 20 June 2024.

8. "Meat and Animal Products." *Greener Pastures*, n.d., togreenerpastures.org. Accessed 20 June 2024.

9. "Industrialization of Agriculture."

10. "Industrialization of Agriculture."

11. John Flesher. "Factory Farms Provide Abundant Food, but Environment Suffers." *PBS*, 6 Feb. 2020, pbs.org. Accessed 5 Aug. 2024.

12. T. Ozbun. "Total Retail and Food Services Sales in the US 1992–2023." *Statista*, 19 Mar. 2024, statista.com. Accessed 20 June 2024.

13. Michael Moss. *Salt, Sugar, Fat: How the Food Giants Hooked Us*. Random House, 2013. 30.

14. "What Are the 11 Diagnostic Criteria in the Yale Food Addiction Scale?" *Examine*, 25 Oct. 2023, examine.com. Accessed 20 June 2024.

CHAPTER 5. THE IMPACTS OF THE FOOD SYSTEM

1. "Food." *United Nations*, n.d., un.org. Accessed 20 June 2024.

2. "Food Insecurity and Nutrition Assistance." *US Department of Agriculture Economic Research Service*, 29 July 2024, ers.usda.gov. Accessed 20 June 2024.

3. Carson Hardee. "New Study Shows Unhealthy Food Advertising Continues to Disproportionately Target Consumers of Color." *UConn Today*, 16 Nov. 2022, today.uconn.edu. Accessed 5 Aug. 2024.

4. Renee Morad. "Can Scientists Create Healthier Foods?" *Scientific American*, 4 Feb. 2019, scientificamerican.com. Accessed 20 June 2024.

5. "Healthy Eating Index 2020." *US Department of Agriculture Food and Nutrition Service*, 14 Sept. 2023, fns.usda.gov. Accessed 5 Aug. 2024.

6. Kristen M. Hurley et al. "The Healthy Eating Index and Youth Healthy Eating Index Are Unique, Nonredundant Measures of Diet Quality among Low-Income, African American Adolescents." *Journal of Nutrition*, vol. 139, no. 2, Feb. 2009, 359–364. *ScienceDirect*, sciencedirect.com. Accessed 5 Aug. 2024.

7. Hannah Ritchie, Pablo Rosado, and Max Roser. "Environmental Impacts of Food Production." *Our World in Data*, 2022, ourworldindata.org. Accessed 5 Aug. 2024.

8. Ritchie, Rosado, and Roser, "Impacts of Food Production."

9. "Americans Poor Diet Drives $50 Billion a Year in Health Care Costs." *National Heart, Lung, and Blood Institute*, 17 Dec. 2019, nhlbi.nih.gov. Accessed 5 Aug. 2024.

10. Katherine D. McManus. "What Are Ultra-Processed Foods and Are They Bad for Our Health?" *Harvard Health Publishing*, 9 Jan. 2020, health.harvard.edu. Accessed 5 Aug. 2024.

CHAPTER 6. FOOD SCIENCE INNOVATIONS

1. "Americans Pick Their Proteins." *University of Minnesota: College of Food, Agricultural and Natural Resource Sciences*, 15 June 2022, cfans.umn.edu. Accessed 5 Aug. 2024.

2. "What Is a Serving?" *American Heart Association*, 26 Mar. 2024, heart.org. Accessed 22 Aug. 2024.

3. Daisy Dunne. "Interactive: What Is the Climate Impact of Eating Meat and Dairy?" *CarbonBrief*, 14 Sept. 2020, interactive.carbonbrief.org. Accessed 22 Aug. 2024.

4. "Future of Food." *Educated Choices Program*, 9 Apr. 2024, learnecprogram.org. Accessed 5 Aug. 2024.

5. "Future of Food."

6. Casey Crownhart. "Here's What We Know about Lab-Grown Meat and Climate Change." *MIT Technology Review*, 3 July 2023, technologyreview.com. Accessed 5 Aug. 2024.

7. Niamh Michail. "Adamo Foods Uses Fermented Mycelium to Replicate Steak Texture." *Global Insights*, 21 Nov. 2023, insights.figlobal.com. Accessed 5 Aug. 2024.

8. "The Science of Plant-Based Meat." *Good Food Institute*, n.d., gfi.org. Accessed 5 Aug. 2024.

9. Emma Ignaszewski. "Plant-Based Meat Is a Significant Growth Opportunity for US and Global Retail and Foodservice." *Good Food Institute*, 11 Apr. 2023, gfi.org. Accessed 5 Aug. 2024.

10. "Genetically Modified Organisms." *National Geographic*, 19 Oct. 2023, education.nationalgeographic.org. Accessed 20 June 2024.

11. "How GMO Technology Saved the Papaya." *Food Insight*, 14 June 2016, foodinsight.org. Accessed 20 June 2024.

12. "The Rise of Superweeds—And What to Do about It." *Union of Concerned Scientists*, Dec. 2013, ucsusa.org. Accessed 20 June 2024.

13. Mary Ellen Kustin. "Glyphosate Is Spreading like a Cancer across the US." *Environmental Working Group*, 7 Apr. 2015, ewg.org. Accessed 20 June 2024.

CHAPTER 7. CAREERS IN FOOD SCIENCE

1. "Food Scientists and Technologists." *My Future*, n.d., myfuture.com. Accessed 20 June 2024.

2. C. Rose Kennedy. "The Flavor Rundown: Natural vs. Artificial Flavors." *Harvard Graduate School of Arts and Sciences*, 21 Sept. 2015, sitn.hms.harvard.edu. Accessed 20 June 2024.

3. Anna Chow Fry. "What Is Sensory Science?" *Peas on Moss*, 21 May 2017, peasonmoss.com. Accessed 20 June 2024.

4. "Space Food: From Creation to Consumption." *Space Center Houston*, 17 Mar. 2020, spacecenter.org. Accessed 20 June 2024.

CHAPTER 8. THE FUTURE OF FOOD SCIENCE

1. Chuck Gill. "Cocoa CRISPR: Gene Editing Shows Promise for Improving the 'Chocolate Tree.'" *Penn State*, 9 May 2018, psu.edu. Accessed 20 June 2024.

2. "Nemo's Garden: The First Ever Underwater Cultivation of Terrestrial Plants." *Nemo's Garden*, May 2023, nemosgarden.com. Accessed 20 June 2024.

3. "Nemo's Garden." *YouTube*, uploaded by OceanReefGroup, n.d., youtube.com. Accessed 5 Aug. 2024.

4. "Nemo's Garden: Underwater Cultivation."

5. "Edible Packaging." *Plastic Smart Cities*, 2 Aug. 2023, plasticsmartcities.org. Accessed 20 June 2024.

6. "Nemo's Garden: Underwater Cultivation."

7. Amanda Hetler. "The Future of the Food Industry: Food Tech Explained." *TechTarget*, 4 Aug. 2022, techtarget.com. Accessed 5 Aug. 2024.

CHRISTA HOGAN

Christa Hogan is an author of many books for kids. She resides in North Carolina, where she also teaches yoga and is raising three teen boys who eat their share of processed foods but get in their fruits and vegetables too.